Heinemann Games Se

WORD GAMES WITH ENGLISH

TEACHER'S RESOURCE BOOK 1

DEIRDRE HOWARD-WILLIAMS & CYNTHIA HERD

REVISED EDITION IN THREE LEVELS

Titles in this series include:

TEACHER'S RESOURCE BOOKS		CLASS BOOKS	
Play Games with English 1	0 435 25016 7	Play Games with English 1	0 435 28060 0
Play Games with English 2	0 435 25017 5	Play Games with English 2	0 435 28062 7
Play Games with English 3	0 435 25018 3		
Word Games with English 1	0 435 25088 4	Word Games with English 1	0 435 28380 4
Word Games with English 2	0 435 25089 2	Word Games with English 2	0 435 28381 2
Word Games with English 3	0 435 25090 6	Word Games with English 3	0 435 28382 0
		Word Games with English Plus	0 435 28379 0
English Puzzles 1	0 435 25084 1	English Puzzles 1	0 435 28280 8
English Puzzles 2	0 435 25085 X	English Puzzles 2	0 435 28281 6
English Puzzles 3	0 435 25086 8	English Puzzles 3	0 435 28282 4
		English Puzzles 4	0 435 28283 2

Heinemann English Language Teaching
A division of Heinemann Publishers (Oxford) Ltd
Halley Court, Jordan Hill, Oxford OX2 8EJ

OXFORD MADRID ATHENS PARIS FLORENCE PRAGUE SÃO PAULO
CHICAGO MELBOURNE AUCKLAND SINGAPORE TOKYO GABORONE
JOHANNESBURG PORTSMOUTH (NH) IBADAN

ISBN 0 435 25088 4

© Deirdre Howard-Williams and Cynthia Herd 1994
First published 1994

PERMISSION TO COPY

The material in this book is copyright. However, the publisher grants permission for copies of pages to be made without fee on those pages marked with the PHOTOCOPIABLE symbol.

Private purchasers may make copies for their own use or for use by classes of which they are in charge; school purchasers may make copies for use within and by the staff and students of the school only. This permission does not extend to additional schools or branches of an institution, who should purchase a separate master copy of the book for their own use.

For copying in any other circumstances, prior permission in writing must be obtained from Heinemann Publishers (Oxford) Ltd.

Illustrated by
Jane Cope and Tony Kenyon

Cover designed by Martin Cox

Teacher's pages designed and typeset by VAP

Dedicated to Sheila Howard-Williams and Barbara Horton Herd

Printed and bound in Great Britain by
Thomson Litho Limited, East Kilbride, Scotland.

93 94 95 96 97 98 10 9 8 7 6 5 4 3 2 1

Contents

N.B. Each game in this list has a brief description given below it. Where there are no descriptions indicating the type of vocabulary used, e.g. doubles, abbreviations etc, the games are of mixed vocabulary, or are self-explanatory.

Introduction	4
Shopping List 1	6
Food Items	
Who?	7
Family Members	
Crossword 1	8
Colours	
Where?	9
Rooms	
The New House	10
Household Items	
Food & Drink	11
In a Café	
Places 1	12
In a Town	
Top Secret	13
Transport	
Holiday List	14
Clothes	
Verb Game 1	15
Activities Word Square	
At the Station	16
Signs	
Abbreviations 1	18
Doubles 1	19
Free Time	20
Activities with -ing	
Legs	21
Numbers	
Opposites 1	22
Adjectives	
Help 1	23
Personal Possessions	
What's the Matter?	24
Health	
At the Hotel	25
Services	
Circle Game	26
Verbs	
Crossword 2	27
Parts of the Body	
Plurals	28
Shopping List 2	29
Quantities	
Doubles 2	30
Verb Game 2	31
Activities Word Square	
What's the Weather like Today?	32
Help 2	33
Hotel Complaints	
Abbreviations 2	34
Places 2	35
Places of Work	
A Business Trip	36
Countries and Currencies	
On the Road	38
Traffic Signs	
Categories Quiz 1	39
All about You	40
Personal Quiz	
Months	41
Opposites 2	42
Adjectives	
Word Families 1	43
Crossword 3	44
Numbers	
Richard's Week	45
Things to Do in Free Time	
Libland	46
Commodities and Quantities	
Word Families 2	48
Opposites 3	49
Phrasal Verbs	
Categories Quiz 2	50
Hands	51
What can you do with them?	
Quick Service	52
Menu Items	
Around the World	53
Countries	
Doubles 3	54
Sports	55
Station Signs	56
Word Families 3	57
Map Reading	58
Meaning of Symbols on a Map	
The Application Form	59
Headings	
A Picnic in the Country	60
Activities with -ing	
Abbreviations 3	61
Opposites 4	62
Crossword 4	63
Prepositions of Position	
Hotel Signs	64
Answers	67
Word List	74

WORD GAMES WITH ENGLISH
Teacher's Introduction

WORD GAMES WITH ENGLISH is a series of three books of carefully graded language activities designed to stimulate learners to practise, activate and extend their English vocabulary.

Each book contains 60 games on photocopiable students' pages plus a full answer key and word list. Each page is highly visual with the words contextualised and their meanings made clear by the illustrations.

Why use games?

Games are an extremely effective way of motivating students in a classroom. Language teachers throughout history have interspersed their grammar or course material with what often seem like lighthearted games, but they do actually touch the language directly and are challenging. And, most importantly perhaps, games are fun!

These resource books are designed to test English vocabulary under the guise of motivating classroom entertainment. You may choose to use them occasionally alongside a standard course or as the basis of a set of needs-orientated one-shot lessons. Each activity could form the core 20 minutes of a vocabulary lesson or maybe the final 20 minutes of a more formal coursebook lesson. For your own reference we have indexed the vocabulary at the back to the page where it occurs.

BOOK 1 is for beginners and post-beginners and contains over 1000 lexical items, allowing the learner to deal with most everyday situations and providing a sound basis for further study. The vocabulary concentrates on the most essential topic areas: personal and family/free time and entertainment/travel/food and drink etc and there is build-in revision and recycling of certain lexical items in different contexts.

BOOK 2 is for intermediate learners who have a general vocabulary of everyday words. By concentrating on a wide variety of up-to-date topics and by developing an awareness of language forms (word building/prefixes and suffixes/prepositional phrases/abbreviations etc) the games enrich and extend this basic vocabulary and enable the learner to understand and express a wider variety of ideas.

BOOK 3 is designed for upper-intermediate learners and corresponds to the standard demanded for the University of Cambridge First Certificate in English, where students are expected to have a good level of general English vocabulary in the 4000 to 5000 word range. Extensive use has been made of authentic materials, such as travel brochures, information booklets and newspapers and special practice has been given in collocation, lexical choice and appropriacy.

Using WORD GAMES WITH ENGLISH in the Classroom

You will find many different types of word games in this book, including crosswords, synonyms, word squares etc and your students will be asked to do different things such as match words and pictures, choose the correct word and fill in blanks.

If you work through the games in order you will find plenty of variety to sustain interest and motivation and your students will benefit from the graded progression and recycling of vocabulary.

However, flexibility is a key feature of WORD GAMES WITH ENGLISH and you may prefer to select games to fill lexical gaps and provide additional practice in a way that will complement other language course material in use. The word list can be used to see where specific vocabulary occurs to enable you to select games of particular interest and relevance to your students' needs.

Students will usually be able to write their answers on the page itself although some games may need extra paper.

Start by making sure that all the students understand exactly what to do. An example is always given so look at this closely. If necessary, do another example with the whole class.

Then the game can either be set for homework to be corrected in a later lesson or can be played in the classroom. Students can work

(i) individually
(ii) in pairs
(iii) in small groups/teams.

You can choose how you do the games, depending on the size of your class and the type of teaching situation. However two ideas are worth bearing in mind.

Generally, those games where the words are all given and then have to be matched either with the correct picture or with another word work well if students try to do as much as they can individually and then compare their work with that of another student, discussing any differences and trying to complete the game between them.

Those games that involve the students in finding the words themselves from a variety of prompts (e.g. crosswords) are often best done in small groups/teams so that knowledge can be pooled and team-work and competition can help them to come up with the answers.

While they are working on the games, walk round the classroom to give help and make suggestions where necessary. Encourage everyone to use English as far as possible and not to give up too easily!

Correction can be done in a variety of ways.

(i) Individual students can exchange their work and correct one another's answers.

(ii) You can call on individual students to come out to the front of the class and say/write their answers for the others to comment on.

(iii) You can ask students (individuals or groups) for their answers and write these on the board.

(iv) You can take the pages in and correct them yourself, giving them back in a later lesson and discussing any problems.

Encourage students to keep the games afterwards as a record and to make a note of all the new vocabulary they have learnt.

Shopping List 1

Look at the shopping. Put the list together.

For example: POT | ATOES = potatoes

WHO?

This is Joe's photo album.
Who is who?

For example: **1** This is my wife and son.

wife and son   grandfather and grandmother   sister
father and mother   brother   dog

CROSSWORD 1
colours

All the answers are colours.

Across

 3 Clouds (sometimes)

 5 Sunset (sometimes)

 6 Sea

 7 Branch of a tree

Down

 1 Snow

 2 Grass

 4 Sun

 7 Night

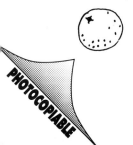 8 An orange

© Deirdre Howard-Williams and Cynthia Herd 1994
HEINEMANN ENGLISH LANGUAGE TEACHING

WHERE?

Jane is phoning the Brown family.
Where are they?

"Hello, is Ann there please?"

For example: **1** She's in the dining room.

2 And Tom?

3 And Frank?

4 And Bob?

5 And Sally?

6 And Pete?

7 And Sue?

dining room   bathroom   garage   bedroom   garden
sitting room   kitchen

© Deirdre Howard-Williams and Cynthia Herd 1994
HEINEMANN ENGLISH LANGUAGE TEACHING

The New House

Mr and Mrs Williams have a new house.
Can you help them put everything in its right place?
Make one list for the kitchen and one for the bedroom.

For example: KITCHEN   BEDROOM
              cup   sheet

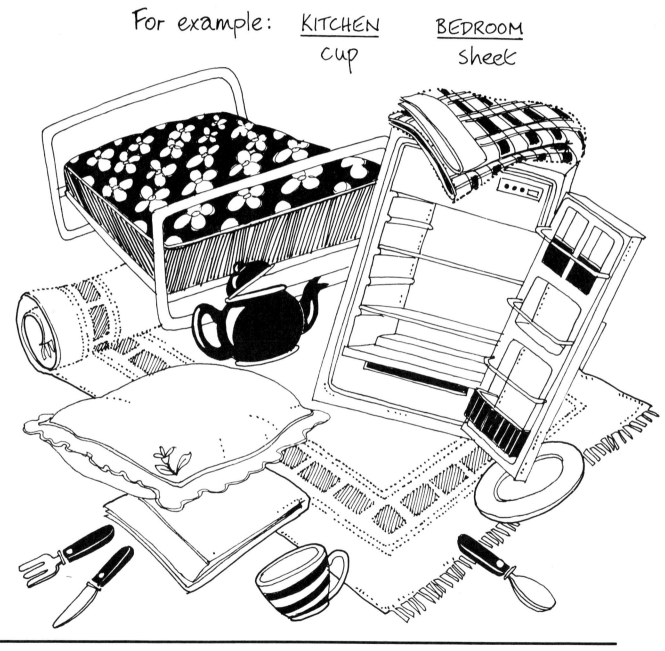

cup   sheet   carpet   fork   bed   knife
plate   fridge   blanket   spoon   pillow   teapot

© Deirdre Howard-Williams and Cynthia Herd 1994
HEINEMANN ENGLISH LANGUAGE TEACHING

Food & Drink

Peter, Diana, Ted and Ruth are in the Quick Food Café. What are they eating?

For example:

DIANA: Soup of the day, omelette, chips, orange juice

PETER: ?

RUTH: ?

TED: ?

soup of the day   omelette   chips   orange juice   beer
roast chicken   cake   chocolate ice-cream   banana
rice   cheese sandwich   biscuits   coffee   wine   tea

PLACES 1

Margaret walked to eight places in this town – first Number 1, then Number 2, etc.
Look at the map and show the way she went.

For example:

1 Hotel
2 Restaurant
3 Bank
4 Church
5 Camping Site
6 Police Station
7 Café
8 Park

TOP SECRET

00001 is a spy.
Read his secret message.

For example:

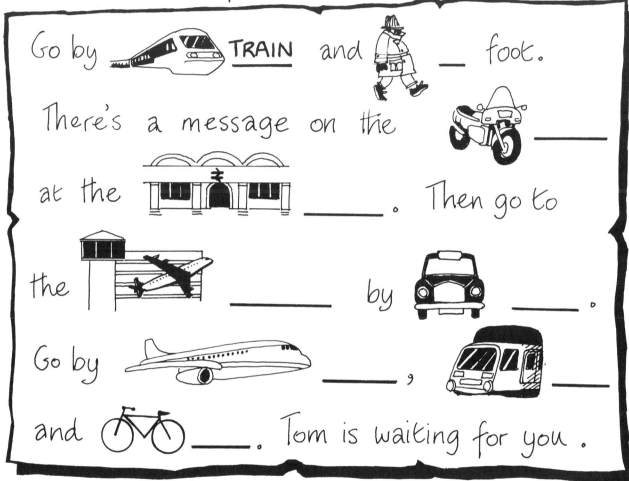

Go by 🚄 TRAIN and 🚶 ___ foot.
There's a message on the 🏍 ___
at the 🚉 ___. Then go to
the ✈🏢 ___ by 🚕 ___.
Go by ✈ ___, 🚐 ___
and 🚲 ___. Tom is waiting for you.

But where is Tom waiting? Look at the message again.

Psst! Look at the first letters again.

T___'_ __ the ____.

underground   plane   train   bicycle   airport
taxi   station   on   motorbike

Holiday List

DON'T FORGET!
- 1 dress ✓
- 1 blouse
- 1 pair of jeans
- 2 pairs of socks
- 1 pair of tights
- underwear
- 1 coat
- 1 jacket
- 1 pullover
- 1 skirt
- 2 pairs of shoes
- passport
- ticket
- camera
- hat

Look at Susie's holiday list.
Can you see it all in her room?

Mark: Yes ✓ or No ✗

© Deirdre Howard-Williams and Cynthia Herd 1994
HEINEMANN ENGLISH LANGUAGE TEACHING

VERB GAME 1

Can you find 10 verbs hidden in this square?
The pictures will help you.
Do this ⌒ or this ( ) .

For example:

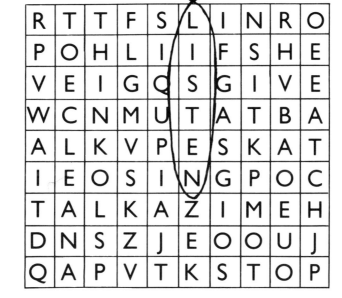

R	T	T	F	S	L	I	N	R	O
P	O	H	L	I	I	F	S	H	E
V	E	I	G	O	S	G	I	V	E
W	C	N	M	U	T	A	T	B	A
A	L	K	V	P	E	S	K	A	T
I	E	O	S	I	N	G	P	O	C
T	A	L	K	A	Z	I	M	E	H
D	N	S	Z	J	E	O	O	U	J
Q	A	P	V	T	K	S	T	O	P

© Deirdre Howard-Williams and Cynthia Herd 1994
HEINEMANN ENGLISH LANGUAGE TEACHING

AT THE STATION

Taxis   Waiting Room   Bar   Danger
Way Out   Platform 1   Closed

Can you put each sign in its correct place?

For example: **1** = Taxis

When you've finished, close the book
and write down all the signs you can remember.
(There are 13.)

Ticket Office   Lost Property Office   Toilets
Open   Travel Centre   Telephone

© Deirdre Howard-Williams and Cynthia Herd 1994
HEINEMANN ENGLISH LANGUAGE TEACHING

ABBREVIATIONS 1

Can you find the correct abbreviations?

For example:

a.m.	ante meridiem (in the morning)
	Great Britain
	pound (weight)
	United States
	please turn over
	metre
	Sunday
	Friday
	north
	Monday
	post meridiem (in the afternoon)
	United States of America
	Saturday
	northeast
	kilometre
	United Kingdom
	Union of Soviet Socialist Republics
	kilogram
	United Nations

doubles 1

Many words in English are made of two words.
Put the word from list A with the correct word from list B.

For example: FIRST NAME

A

FIRST
DEPARTURE
TELEPHONE
BUS
CAMPING
SHOPPING
ORANGE
GROUND
TELEPHONE

B

JUICE
FLOOR
SITE
LOUNGE
BOX
STATION
NUMBER
NAME
LIST

Free Time

Mr Jones and Mrs Smith have many interests. Write two lists.

← For example →

Mr. Jones — dancing
Mrs. Smith — walking

---

dancing   walking   learning foreign languages
driving   watching television   cooking   swimming
playing football   reading   listening to music

LEGS

Count the number of legs

For example:

Three dogs	twelve	Legs 12
Four cats		Legs
One farmer & two horses		Legs
One bird		Legs
One fly		Legs
One tourist guide & fourteen tourists		Legs
Two chairs		Legs
Four tables		Legs
Mr & Mrs Brown & their three daughters		Legs
Total		Legs

If you are right, the total is the same as the number of legs in five football teams.

© Deirdre Howard-Williams and Cynthia Herd 1994
HEINEMANN ENGLISH LANGUAGE TEACHING

opposites 1

Here are 7 pairs of adjectives.
Can you find the correct pictures?
Write the numbers beside the words.

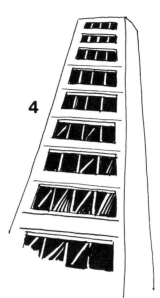

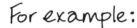

For example:

9	Dark	Light	1
	Cheap	Expensive	
	Quiet	Noisy	
	High	Low	
	Old	New	
	Young	Old	
	Heavy	Light	

© Deirdre Howard-Williams and Cynthia Herd 1994
HEINEMANN ENGLISH LANGUAGE TEACHING

HELP 1

Jack and Sally are staying at the same hotel. He is on holiday and she is a journalist. Today he is going to the beach and she is working. Can you say what is his and what is hers?

For example: HERS - money
             HIS - ball

money   ball   bottle of water   map   boat
book   car keys   notebook   sunglasses
pen   towel   hat   cheque book   radio

What's the matter?

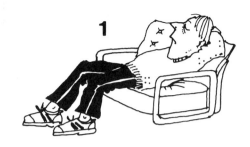

Look at him... he's not happy, is he?
Can you say why?
Fill in the missing words.

For example: **1** He's tired.

2 He's .... on the .....

3 He's got a .....

4 He's ....

5 He's ....

6 He's ..... his ....

7 He's .... his ....

8 He's got a ....
in his ....

9 He's .... his ....

10 He's ......

---

tired	fallen	pain	ill	broken	ice	finger
cold	thirsty	burnt	arm	hand	hungry	
cut	back					

AT THE HOTEL

Look at the list. Can you give each service its name?

THE RITZ HOTEL: OUR SERVICES FOR GUESTS

For example:

1. BREAKFAST — from 6.30 a.m. to 10.30 a.m.
2. _____ — open for lunch and dinner
3. _____ — for drinks till 11.30 p.m.
4. _____ — dial '0' for Reception
5. _____ — for Traveller's Cheques only
6. _____ — in Emergency ask at Reception
7. _____ — in every room
8. _____ — in double rooms only
9. _____ — free for guests' cars
10. _____ — at 12.00 (midday)
11. _____ — can be guests too for £1 a day
12. _____ — tell us the night before

Breakfast   Television   Dogs   Change   Restaurant
Bar   Check-out   Doctor   Radio   Wake-up
Telephone   Parking

© Deirdre Howard-Williams and Cynthia Herd 1994
HEINEMANN ENGLISH LANGUAGE TEACHING

CIRCLE GAME

Find the object and then find the correct verb.

For example: pay a bill

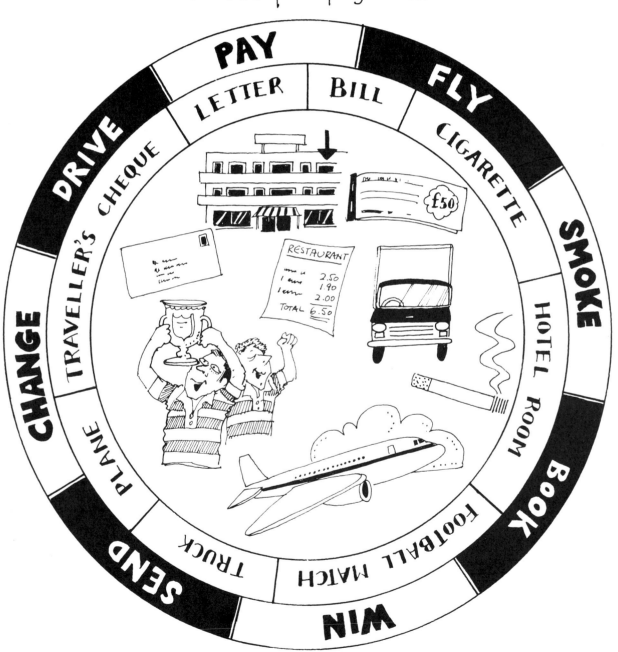

CROSSWORD 2
the body

All the answers are parts of the body.

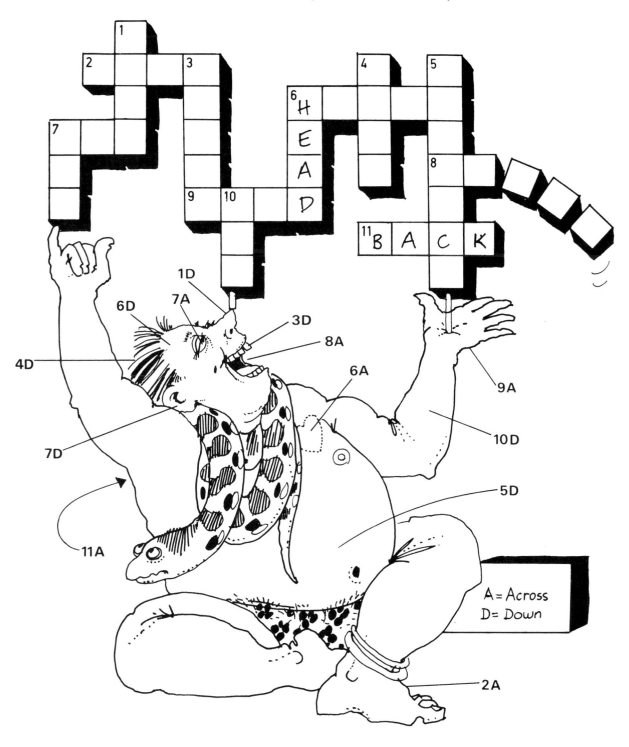

A = Across
D = Down

Plurals

Look at the singular form and write the plural.

For example: 1 women

woman   tooth   leaf   comb   bus   foot   watch
flower   child   policeman   island   car   knife   glass
factory

Shopping List 2

Look at the shopping Mike has brought home. Write his list.

For example: **1** a kilo of beans

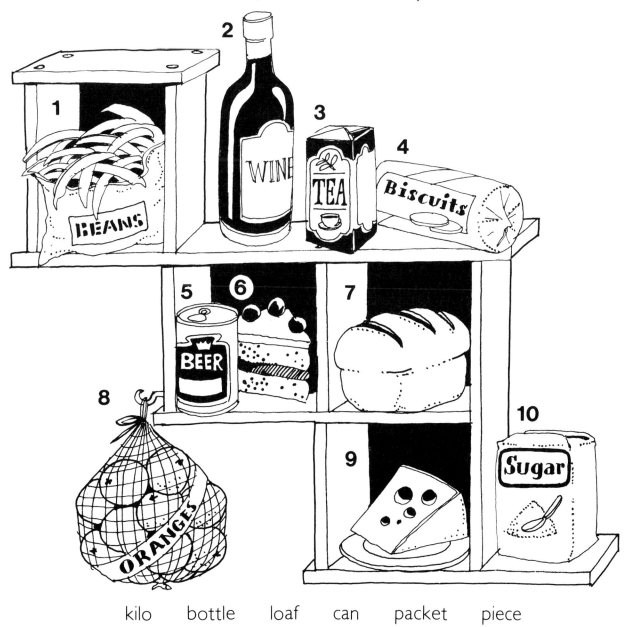

kilo   bottle   loaf   can   packet   piece

doubles 2

Many words in English are made of two parts.
Put the word from list A with the correct word from list B.

For example: TOOTHPASTE, COFFEE-POT

A
TOOTH
COFFEE-
WEEK
FOOT
LIVING
HAIR
MOTOR
TOOTH
BATH
ICE-
BED
POST

B
CREAM
END
CARD
ROOM
POT
BIKE
PASTE
BALL
CUT
ROOM
BRUSH
ROOM

VERB GAME 2

Can you find 10 verbs hidden in this square?
The pictures will help you.
Do this ⌒ or this ◯.

For example:

I	R	W	A	L	K	A	K	G	A
R	I	V	P	E	M	T	C	H	J
Q	D	A	R	A	U	T	P	B	Z
S	E	O	N	V	W	Y	R	U	N
D	A	N	C	E	C	L	A	F	B
T	E	D	X	G	O	F	B	I	H
S	W	I	M	Z	M	L	C	U	K
A	R	R	I	V	E	Y	A	E	Q

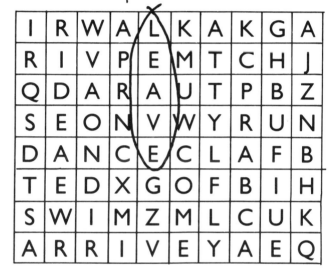

© Deirdre Howard-Williams and Cynthia Herd 1994
HEINEMANN ENGLISH LANGUAGE TEACHING

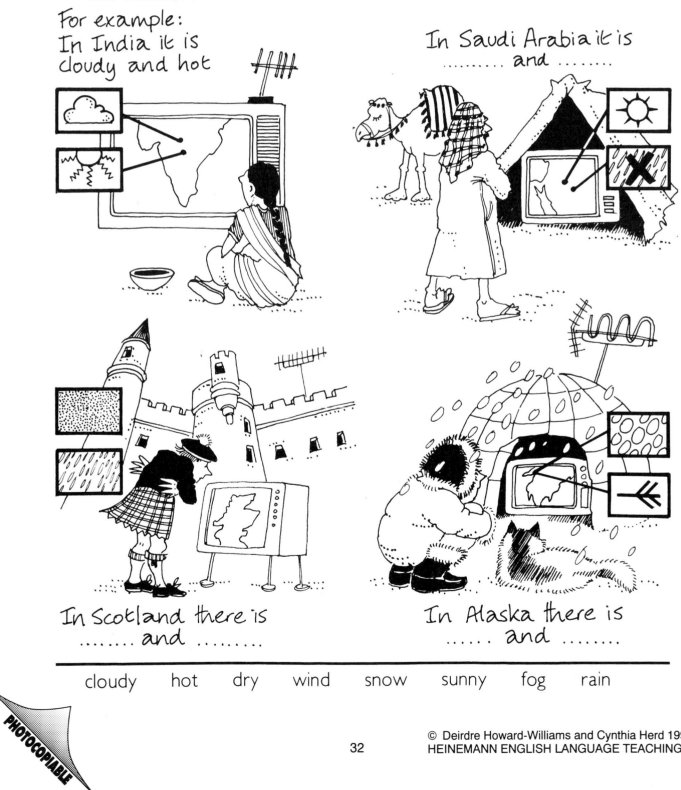

HELP 2

Mr & Mrs Davies are staying at the Sunny Days Hotel. Say what's missing.

For example: **1** There's no water.

water   chair   pillow   key   heating   knife and fork
lift   light   towel

ABBREVIATIONS 2

Can you find the correct abbreviations?

For example:

Dec.	December
	Before Christ
	Parking
	Postscript
	south
	telephone
	television
	Avenue
	Square
	Doctor
	nota bene (take special note of)
	southwest
	Street
	water closet (toilet)
	Road
	anno Domini (in the year of our Lord)
	week
	pence
	year

PHOTOCOPIABLE

© Deirdre Howard-Williams and Cynthia Herd 1994
HEINEMANN ENGLISH LANGUAGE TEACHING

PLACES 2

Tom is old now. When he was younger he worked in many different places. Where?

For example:
1 He worked in a market.

market   hospital   post office   cinema
factory   supermarket   ticket office   office

A Business Trip

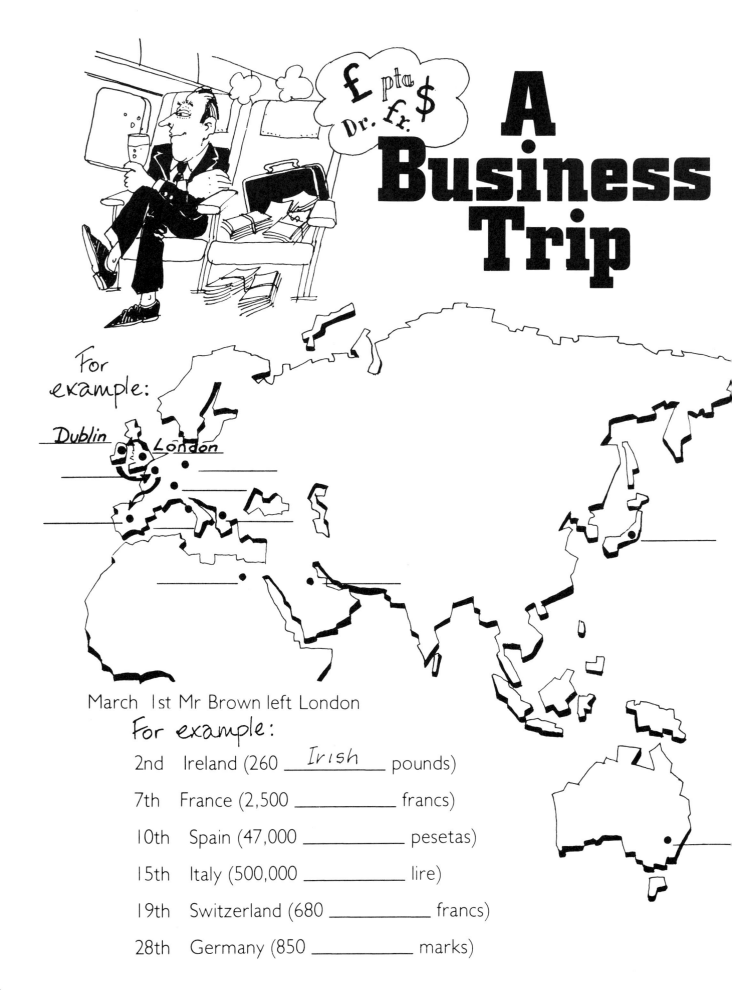

For example:

Dublin — London

March 1st Mr Brown left London

For example:

2nd   Ireland (260 ___Irish___ pounds)

7th   France (2,500 _____ francs)

10th   Spain (47,000 _____ pesetas)

15th   Italy (500,000 _____ lire)

19th   Switzerland (680 _____ francs)

28th   Germany (850 _____ marks)

© Deirdre Howard-Williams and Cynthia Herd 1994
HEINEMANN ENGLISH LANGUAGE TEACHING

Last spring Mr Brown went round the world on a business trip. Show on the map the way he went and name the capital cities he visited.
Fill in the blanks to show what money he spent.

April 3rd Greece
(27,000 _____ drachmas)

10th Saudi Arabia
(1,100 _____ riyals)

17th Egypt
(300 _____ pounds)

24th Australia
(360 _____ dollars)

30th Japan
(77,400 _____ yen)

May 5th Canada
(400 _____ dollars)

14th Mexico
(60,200 _____ pesos)

22nd Brazil
(83,000 _____ cruzeiros)

31st Back to London.

Brasilia
Mexico City
Dublin
London
Bonn
Paris
Geneva
Madrid
Rome
Athens
Cairo
Ottowa
Tokyo
Canberra
Riyadh

on the road

Do you know these traffic signs?
For example: **1** No stopping

No stopping   Children   No entry   Sheep
No right turn No walking   Traffic lights
No cycling   Men at work No left turn   Picnic site

CATEGORIES QUIZ 1

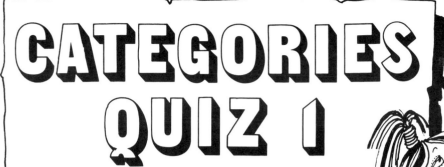

Put a ☒ next to the correct answer.

For example:

1. *Susan* is a
   a surname ☐
   b first name ☒
   c boy's name ☐

2. *France* is a
   a language ☐
   b nationality ☐
   c country ☐

3. *A station* is a
   a train ☐
   b place ☐
   c country ☐

4. *A supermarket* is a
   a job ☐
   b shop ☐
   c farm ☐

5. *Coffee* is a
   a meal ☐
   b drink ☐
   c place ☐

6. *A fly* is an
   a insect ☐
   b aeroplane ☐
   c airport ☐

7. *A kitchen* is a
   a room ☐
   b sport ☐
   c shop ☐

8. *Eight* is a
   a number ☐
   b colour ☐
   c date ☐

9. *A teacher* is a
   a job ☐
   b person ☐
   c school ☐

10. *March* is a
    a day ☐
    b holiday ☐
    c month ☐

© Deirdre Howard-Williams and Cynthia Herd 1994
HEINEMANN ENGLISH LANGUAGE TEACHING

all about YOU

Judy is doing a quiz. Look at the pictures and fill in the answers for her.

1

2

3

What Sort of Person are YOU??

Answer these questions and see.

For example:

1. How do you eat?
   ☐ slowly   ☒ quickly
2. How do you sleep?
   ☐ well   ☐ badly
3. How much do you read?
   ☐ a little   ☐ a lot
4. Are you ever late for work?
   ☐ always   ☐ never
5. When do you get up?
   ☐ early   ☐ late
6. Which season do you prefer for holidays?
   ☐ summer   ☐ winter

4

5

6

© Deirdre Howard-Williams and Cynthia Herd 1994
HEINEMANN ENGLISH LANGUAGE TEACHING

Months

Can you find the correct month?

For example:

1. July   takes its name from Julius Caesar.
2. ...... has the fewest days.
3. ...... is the longest (number of letters).

4. ...... has Christmas on the twenty-fifth.
5. ...... has thirty days and eight letters.
6. ...... starts with the letter O.

7. ...... has the letter I at the end.
8. ...... is a holiday for students in Britain.
9. ...... is the first month.

10. ...... is the shortest (number of letters).
11. ...... is also a verb (soldiers do it).
12. ...... is also a girl's name.

© Deirdre Howard-Williams and Cynthia Herd 1994
HEINEMANN ENGLISH LANGUAGE TEACHING

opposites 2

Here are 7 pairs of adjectives.
Can you find the correct pictures?

1

2

3

For example:

1	Easy	Difficult	11
	Right	Wrong	
	Big	Small	
	Fat	Thin	
	Soft	Hard	
	Fast	Slow	
	Tall	Short	

4

5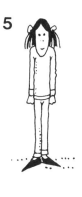

6

7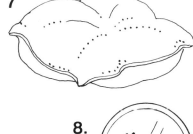

8

9

10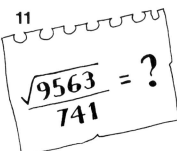

11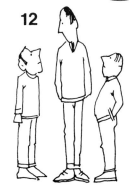

12

13

14

PHOTOCOPIABLE

© Deirdre Howard-Williams and Cynthia Herd 1994
HEINEMANN ENGLISH LANGUAGE TEACHING

Word Families 1

Which word is different from the others?

For example:

1. Road
   River ✗
   Street
   Square

2. Book
   Magazine
   Television
   Newspaper

3. Arm
   Head
   Hand
   Hat

4. Eggs
   Salt
   Pepper
   Mustard

5. Gallon
   Bottle
   Litre
   Pint

6. Boss
   Wife
   Son
   Daughter

7. Doctor
   Medicine
   Taxi
   Ambulance

8. Postcard
   Stamp
   Letter
   Travellers' cheques

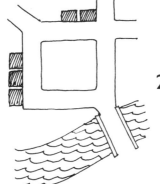

© Deirdre Howard-Williams and Cynthia Herd 1994
HEINEMANN ENGLISH LANGUAGE TEACHING

CROSSWORD 3
numbers

All the answers are numbers.

Across →

1	13	11	½
3	40	13	1x
5	1ST	15	2
7	10	17	12
9	2ND	18	0

Down ↓

1	3RD	9	60
2	9	10	90
4	2x	12	4
6	6	14	11
8	¼	16	1

© Deirdre Howard-Williams and Cynthia Herd 1994
HEINEMANN ENGLISH LANGUAGE TEACHING

Richard's Week

Fill in what Richard is going to do this week. For example:

cinema   good news programme on the radio   party
football   book tickets for the theatre   out with friends
Arabic class

Libland sells
1. a lot of …
2. a few …
3. a little …
4. a little …
5. a lot of …
6. a little …

Libland doesn't sell
7. much …
8. many …
9. much …

For example:
1. Libland sells a lot of wood.

For example:
7. Libland doesn't sell much coffee.

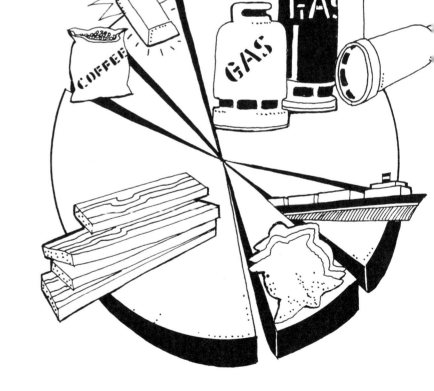

wood leather gold
ships coffee gas

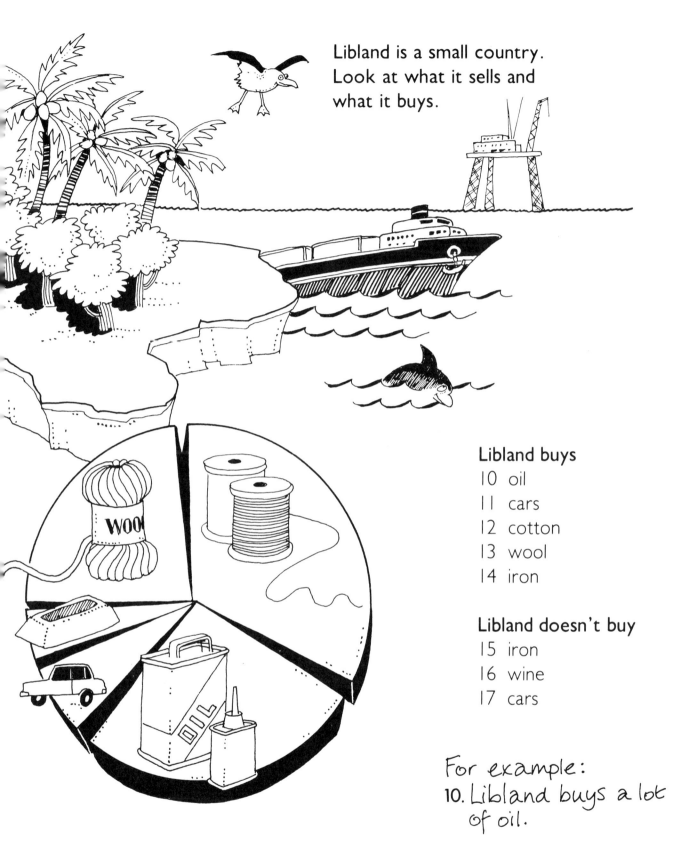

Libland is a small country. Look at what it sells and what it buys.

Libland buys
10 oil
11 cars
12 cotton
13 wool
14 iron

Libland doesn't buy
15 iron
16 wine
17 cars

For example:
10. Libland buys a lot of oil.

For example:
15. Libland doesn't buy much iron.

a lot of   much   a few
a little   many   any

Word Families 2

Language · Signs · Picnic places
Occupations · Hotel · Shopping

Put these words into their correct families.
There are 4 in each.

speak   pronounce   understand   mean   size   lake
nylon   reception   dentist   exit   student   try on
hill   entrance   shop assistant   beach   nurse   how much?
single room   pull   fields   push   double room   bill

For example: LANGUAGE
speak, pronounce, understand, mean

opposites 3

Can you find the 6 pairs of verbs?

For example:
1 Come in and go out

come in   go out   take off   ask   win   put on
sleep   answer   lose   get up   wake up   go to bed

CATEGORIES QUIZ 2

Put a ☒ next to the correct answer.

For example:

1. *Russian* is a
   - a place ☐
   - b nationality ☒
   - c job ☐

2. *Trousers* are
   - a clothes ☐
   - b money ☐
   - c food ☐

3. *Dr* is an abbreviation for
   - a December ☐
   - b Doctor ☐
   - c dear ☐

4. *Swimming* is a
   - a place ☐
   - b fish ☐
   - c sport ☐

5. *Mrs Brown* is
   - a a child ☐
   - b married ☐
   - c not married ☐

6. *Michael* is a
   - a woman's name ☐
   - b surname ☐
   - c man's name ☐

7. *A banana* is a
   - a fruit ☐
   - b vegetable ☐
   - c meal ☐

8. *The Nile* is a
   - a sea ☐
   - b river ☐
   - c mountain ☐

9. *The finger* is a
   - a room ☐
   - b time ☐
   - c part of the body ☐

© Deirdre Howard-Williams and Cynthia Herd 1994
HEINEMANN ENGLISH LANGUAGE TEACHING

HANDS

What can you do with your hands?

For example: 1. turn on

turn on   make   steal   wash   buy   break   drive
turn off   write   cut

QUICK SERVICE

This waiter is carrying 8 different dishes for 8 different people. The number on each dish is the number of the order. Can you fill in his orders?

For example:

roast pork and peas   grilled lamb, mushrooms and peas
spaghetti with tomato sauce   ham salad and bread roll
fried bacon and sausages   strawberries and cream
boiled beef, carrots and cabbage   vanilla ice-cream and pears

AROUND THE WORLD

Can you recognise these countries?
Can you spell them correctly?

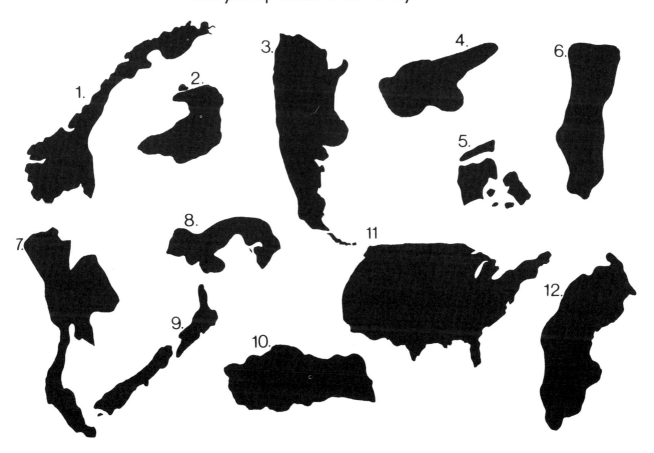

For example:

1. RYNOAW   Norway
2. ASEWL
3. TANGRIANE
4. PYSUCR
5. KANDERM
6. APUGRTOL
7. HALITNAD
8. APAMNA
9. EWN LAZENDA
10. YURTEK
11. IDENUT TESAST
12. DESWEN

© Deirdre Howard-Williams and Cynthia Herd 1994
HEINEMANN ENGLISH LANGUAGE TEACHING

Can you name these sports and write them in the correct column?

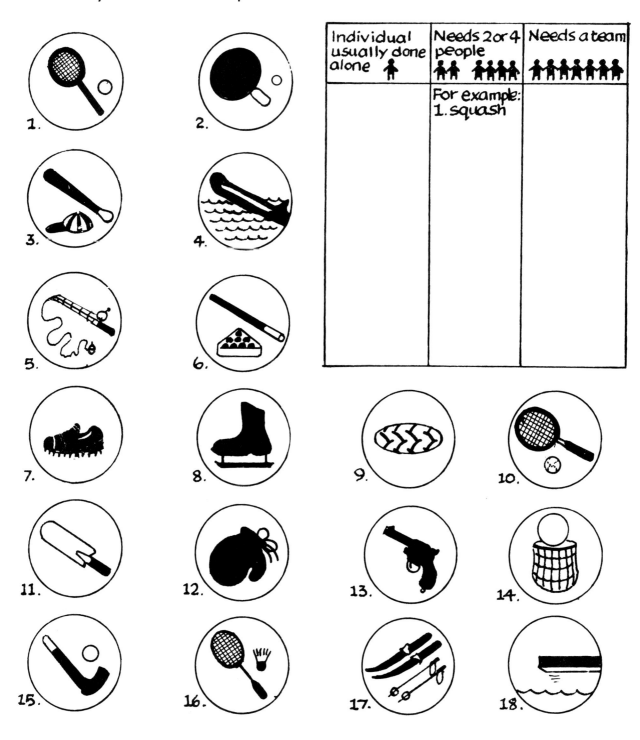

squash   skiing   boxing   table tennis   rugby   tennis   badminton
basketball   running   hockey   baseball   water-skiing   snooker
fishing   shooting   diving   ice skating   cricket

Station Signs

All these signs can be seen at railway stations.
Can you find the word or words to explain these signs?

  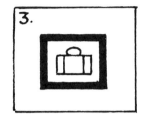 

For example: 1. luggage lockers

Number		
1.	luggage	cafeteria
	information	lockers
	buffet	property
	lost	room
	facilities	water
	meeting	telephone
	waiting	and washroom
	luggage	for the
	public	handicapped
	left	rental
	car	smokers
	toilets	trolleys
	non-drinking	point
		luggage

    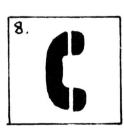

© Deirdre Howard-Williams and Cynthia Herd 1994
HEINEMANN ENGLISH LANGUAGE TEACHING

Word Families 3

Here are 24 words. Can you put them into 6 different subject groups?

saucer pair frost dozen pot wound minister party member
directory call box thunderstorm disease socialist fever operator
billion dish injury lightning communist couple pan gale dial

For example:
saucer
_____

Map Reading

Look at the map. What do the symbols represent?
Complete the key.

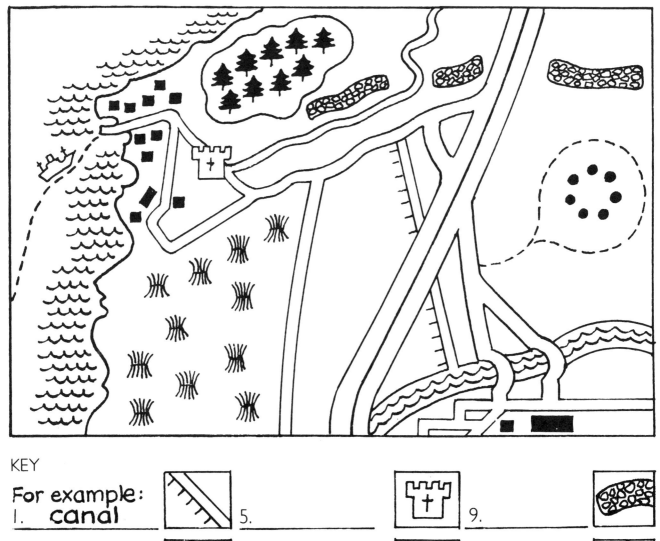

KEY

For example:
1. canal

2. _____
3. _____
4. _____
5. _____
6. _____
7. _____
8. _____
9. _____
10. _____
11. _____
12. _____

canal   farmland   motorway   footpath   coast   old wall
ferry   stone circle   village   forest   bridge   castle

The Application Form

Jane Anderson has filled in this application for a new job. You have her answers. Can you finish the form?

```
APPLICATION FORM
Please type or write clearly.
For Example                                    2. _____ Ms.
1. FAMILY NAME  Anderson
3. _____ Jane Irene
4. _____ 30th July 1961      5. _____ York
6. _____ Single                        7. _____ None
8. _____ 27 Glenhill Gardens, Richmond
                  Surrey              9. _____ 584-29-01
10. _____ York Girls' School '72-'79
11. _____ Raydon College of Art '79-'83
                  Diploma in Art and Design (DIP AD) '83
12. _____ Art and Craft Summer School (Assistant
                  Teacher) Spain '83 + '84
                  Art Department I.Y.C. magazine
13. _____ £ 8,500 P.A.
14. _____ French and Spanish, German (a little)
15. _____ Yes
16. _____ Photography, Astronomy, Mountain
17. _____ Climbing
                  Ignacio Ibañez        S. Warlock
18. _____ 430.5. 4° Calle Muñoz   Art Director
                  Tarragona, Spain      22 Bedhill Place
                  from January 1st '86
19. _____ Nov. 15th '85.    21 _____
20. _____                      Jane Anderson
```

Family name   Interests   Tel. no.   Education: schools attended   Signature
Marital status   Languages spoken   Names and addresses of 2 referees
First names   Place of birth   Education: university/college   Mr/Mrs/Miss/Ms
Date available   Date   Present address   Children   Driving licence
Present position   Date of birth   Present salary   Previous experience

© Deirdre Howard-Williams and Cynthia Herd 1994
HEINEMANN ENGLISH LANGUAGE TEACHING

A Picnic in the Country

Look at this busy scene in the country. What are people doing? Answer with TRUE or FALSE.

For example:

	True	False
1. Someone's reading.	X	
2. Someone's swimming.		X
3. Someone's driving.		
4. Someone's climbing.		
5. Someone's drinking.		
6. Someone's riding.		
7. Someone's resting.		
8. Someone's fighting.		
9. Someone's jumping.		
10. Someone's sewing.		

	True	False
11. Someone's crying.		
12. Someone's shaving.		
13. Someone's hurrying.		
14. Someone's laughing.		
15. Someone's hiding.		
16. Someone's standing.		
17. Someone's leaving.		
18. Someone's shooting.		
19. Someone's watching.		
20. Someone's running.		

© Deirdre Howard-Williams and Cynthia Herd 1994
HEINEMANN ENGLISH LANGUAGE TEACHING

ABBREVIATIONS 3

Do you understand these abbreviations? Write them out in full

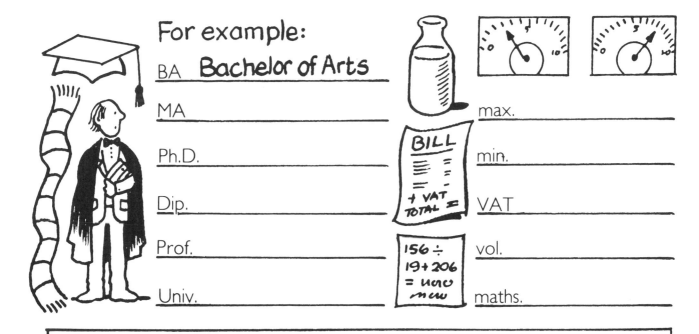

For example:

BA __Bachelor of Arts__

MA _____

Ph.D. _____

Dip. _____

Prof. _____

Univ. _____

max. _____

min. _____

VAT _____

vol. _____

maths. _____

Bachelor of Arts   Limited   minimum   Headquarters   volume
Value Added Tax   miles per gallon   Professor   maximum
European Economic Community (Common Market)   Captain
Company   mathematics   Doctor of Philosophy   England   Diploma
government   miles per hour   Master of Arts   University   British Airways

---

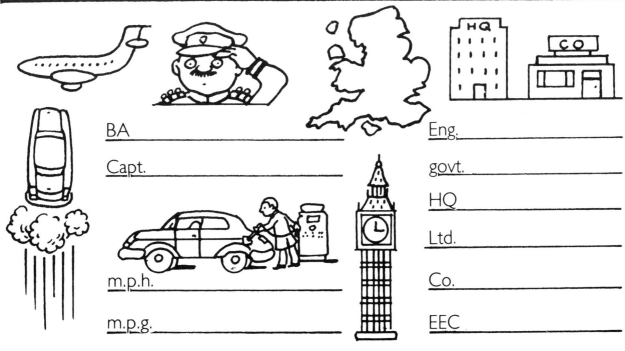

BA _____

Capt. _____

m.p.h. _____

m.p.g. _____

Eng. _____

govt. _____

HQ _____

Ltd. _____

Co. _____

EEC _____

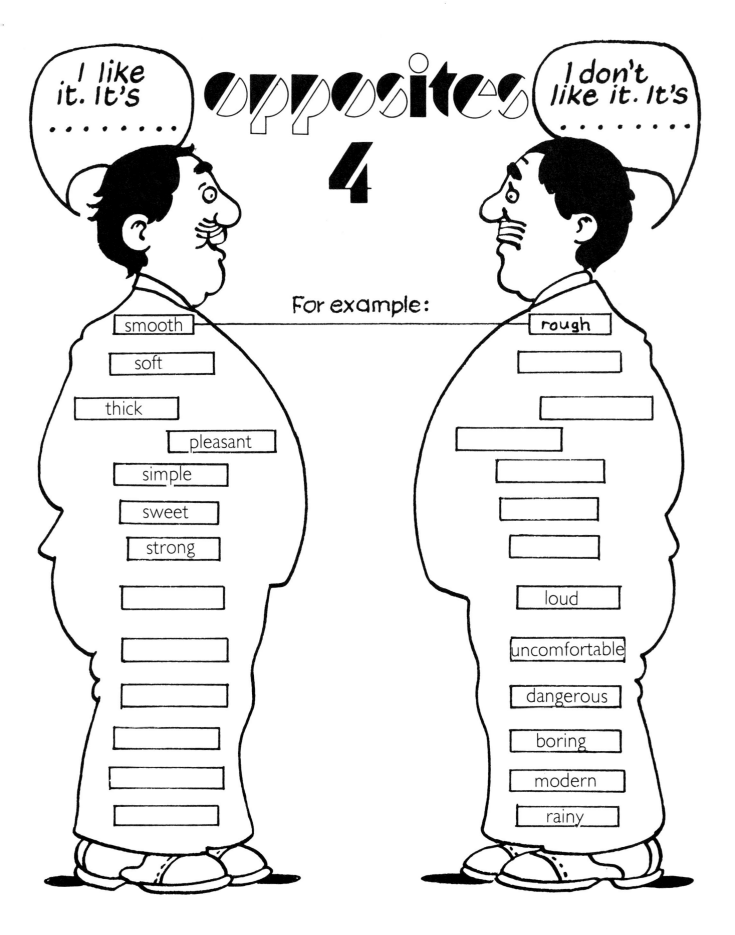

rough interesting hard thin weak bitter fine
difficult unpleasant safe comfortable soft antique

CROSSWORD 4

All the answers are connected with **position**. Use the rabbit to help you.

Across: →

Down: ↓

Hotel

Can you put each sign in its correct place?

For example: 1. Ring for service

Ring for service   Porter   Lounge   Please do not disturb   Swimming pool   Tours

Messages for guests   Manager   Roof garden   Check in here   Laundry   Luggage

Answers

Shopping List 1
Page 6

Potatoes, fish, milk, bread, cheese, butter, apples, meat.

Who?
Page 7

1. This is my wife and son.
2. This is my father and mother.
3. This is my grandfather and grandmother.
4. This is my brother.
5. This is my sister.
6. This is my dog.

Crossword 1 – Colours
Page 8

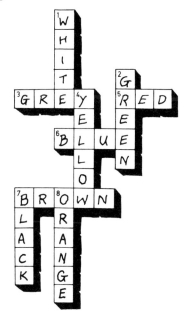

Where?
Page 9

1. She's in the dining room.
2. He's in the sitting room.
3. He's in the bathroom.
4. He's in the garden.
5. She's in the bedroom.
6. He's in the garage.
7. She's in the kitchen.

The New House
Page 10

Kitchen: cup, fork, knife, plate, fridge, spoon, teapot
Bedroom: sheet, carpet, bed, blanket, pillow

Food and Drink
Page 11

Diana: soup of the day, omelette, chips, orange juice
Peter: cake, biscuits, tea
Ruth: cheese sandwich, banana, beer
Ted: roast chicken, rice, wine, chocolate ice-cream, coffee

Places 1
Page 12

1	Hotel
2	Restaurant
3	Bank
4	Church
5	Camping Site
6	Police Station
7	Café
8	Park

Top Secret
Page 13

Train, On (foot), Motorbike, Station, Airport, Taxi, Plane, Underground, Bicycle. TOM'S AT THE PUB

Holiday List
Page 14

Verb Game 1

Page 15

```
R T T F S L I N R O
P O H L I F S H E E
V E I G Q S G I V E
W C N M U T A T B A
A L K V P E S K A T
I E O S I N G P O C
T A L K A Z I M E H
D N S Z J E O O U J
Q A P V T K S T O P
```

At the Station

Page 16

1. Taxis
2. Way Out
3. Toilets
4. Telephones
5. Platform 1
6. Danger
7. Bar
8. Travel Centre
9. Closed
10. Ticket Office
11. Waiting Room
12. Lost Property Office
13. Open

Abbreviations 1

Page 18

a.m.	ante meridiem (in the morning)
G.B.	Great Britain
lb	pound (weight)
US	United States
PTO.	please turn over
m	metre
Sun.	Sunday
Fri.	Friday
N.	north
Mon.	Monday
p.m.	post meridiem (in the afternoon)
USA	United States of America
Sat.	Saturday
NE	northeast
Km	kilometre
UK	United Kingdom
USSR	Union of Soviet Socialist Republics
Kg	kilogram
U.N	United Nations

Doubles 1

Page 19

first name, departure lounge, telephone box, bus station, camping site, shopping list, orange juice, ground floor, telephone number

Free Time

Page 20

Mr Jones: dancing, playing football, reading, cooking, watching television

Mrs Smith: walking, learning foreign languages, driving, swimming, listening to music

Legs

Page 21

Three dogs	twelve	Legs	12
Four cats	sixteen	Legs	16
One farmer & two horses	ten	Legs	10
One bird	two	Legs	2
One fly	six	Legs	6
One tourist guide & fourteen tourists	thirty	Legs	30
Two chairs	eight	Legs	8
Four tables	sixteen	Legs	16
Mr & Mrs Brown & their three daughters	ten	Legs	10
Total	One hundred and ten	Legs	110

Opposites 1

Page 22

9	Dark	Light	1
2	Cheap	Expensive	8
3	Quiet	Noisy	10
4	High	Low	14
6	Old	New	12
7	Young	Old	13
11	Heavy	Light	5

Help

Page 23

Hers: money, map, car keys, notebook, pen, cheque book

His: ball, bottle of water, boat, book, sunglasses, hat, radio, towel

What's the Matter?

Page 24

1. He's tired.
2. He's fallen on the ice.
3. He's got a cold.
4. He's thirsty.
5. He's hungry.
6. He's cut his finger.
7. He's broken his arm.
8. He's got a pain in his back.
9. He's burnt his hand.
10. He's ill.

At the Hotel

Page 25

1. Breakfast
2. Restaurant
3. Bar
4. Telephone
5. Change
6. Doctor
7. Radio
8. Television
9. Parking
10. Check-out
11. Dogs
12. Wake-up

Circle Game

Page 26

Pay a bill, fly a plane, smoke a cigarette, book a hotel room, win a football match, send a letter, change a traveller's cheque, drive a truck

Crossword 2 – The Body
Page 27

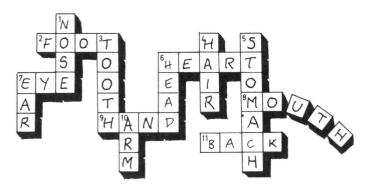

Plurals
Page 28

1. Women
2. Cars
3. Buses
4. Knives
5. Teeth
6. Combs
7. Feet
8. Children
9. Watches
10. Policemen
11. Islands
12. Leaves
13. Glasses
14. Flowers
15. Factories

Shopping List 2
Page 29

1. A kilo of beans
2. A bottle of wine
3. A packet of tea
4. A packet of biscuits
5. A can of beer
6. A piece of cake
7. A loaf of bread
8. A kilo of oranges
9. A piece of cheese
10. A packet of sugar

Doubles 2
Page 30

toothpaste, coffee-pot, weekend, football, livingroom, haircut, motorbike, toothbrush, bathroom, ice-cream, bedroom, postcard

Verb Game 2
Page 31

I	R	W	A	L	K	A	K	G	A
R	I	V	P	E	M	T	C	H	J
Q	D	A	R	A	U	T	P	B	Z
S	E	O	N	V	W	Y	R	U	N
D	A	N	C	E	C	L	A	F	B
T	E	D	X	G	O	F	B	I	H
S	W	I	M	Z	M	L	C	U	K
A	R	R	I	V	E	Y	A	E	Q

What's the Weather Like Today?
Page 32

In India it is cloudy and hot.
In Saudi Arabia it is dry and sunny.
In Scotland there is rain and fog.
In Alaska there is snow and wind.

Help 2
Page 33

1. There's no water.
2. There's no lift.
3. There's no key.
4. There's no light.
5. There's no towel.
6. There's no heating.
7. There's no chair.
8. There's no pillow.
9. There's no knife and fork.

Abbreviations 2
Page 34

Dec.	December
BC	Before Christ
P	Parking
P.S.	Postscript
S.	south
tel.	telephone
TV	television
Ave.	Avenue
Sq.	Square
Dr.	Doctor
NB	nota bene (take special note of)
SW	southwest
St.	Street
W.C	water closet (toilet)
Rd.	Road
AD	anno Domini (in the year of our Lord)
wk	week
p.	pence
yr.	year

Places 2
Page 35

1. He worked in a market.
2. He worked in a factory.
3. He worked in a cinema.
4. He worked in a supermarket.
5. He worked in a post office.
6. He worked in an office.
7. He worked in a ticket office.
8. He worked in a hospital.

A Business Trip

Page 36

March 2nd Irish, 7th French, 10th Spanish, 15th Italian, 19th Swiss, 28th German, April 3rd Greek, 10th Saudi, 17th Egyptian, 24th Australian, 30th Japanese, May 5th Canadian, 14th Mexican, 22nd Brazilian

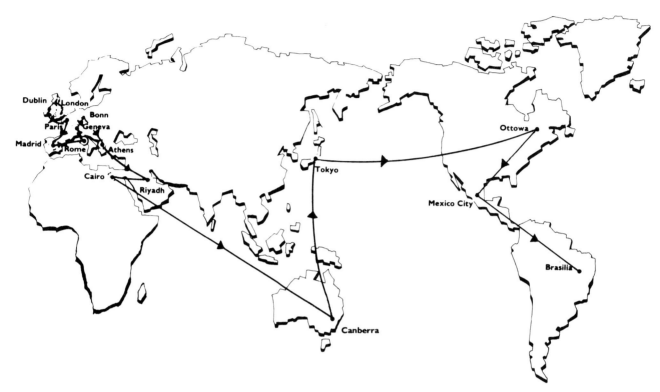

On the Road

Page 38

1. No stopping
2. Sheep
3. No cycling
4. Traffic lights
5. Men at work
6. Picnic site
7. No right turn
8. No walking
9. No left turn
10. No entry
11. Children

Categories Quiz 1

Page 39

1b, 2c, 3b, 4b, 5b, 6a, 7a, 8a, 9b, 10c

All About You

Page 40

1. quickly
2. well
3. a lot
4. always
5. early
6. winter

Months

Page 41

1. July
2. February
3. September
4. December
5. November
6. October
7. April
8. August
9. January
10. May
11. March
12. June

Opposites 2

Page 42

For example:

1	Easy	Difficult	11
2	Right	Wrong	13
14	Big	Small	8
6	Fat	Thin	5
7	Soft	Hard	9
4	Fast	Slow	3
12	Tall	Short	10

Word Families 1

Page 43

1. river
2. television
3. hat
4. eggs
5. bottle
6. boss
7. taxi
8. traveller's cheques

Crossword 3 – Numbers

Page 44

Richard's Week

Page 45

Monday 28th: 8 p.m. cinema
Tuesday 29th: 11 a.m. book tickets for the theatre
Wednesday 30th: 7.30 p.m. out with friends
Thursday 1st: 3 p.m. Arabic class
Friday 2nd: 10 p.m. party
Saturday 3rd: 2.15 p.m. football
Sunday 4th: 1 p.m. good news programme on the radio

Libland

Page 46

1. Libland sells a lot of wood.
2. Libland sells a few ships.
3. Libland sells a little coffee, leather, gold.
4. Libland sells a little leather, coffee, gold.
5. Libland sells a lot of gas.
6. Libland sells a little gold, leather, coffee.
7. Libland doesn't sell much coffee, leather, gold.
8. Libland doesn't sell many ships.
9. Libland doesn't sell much leather, coffee, gold.
10. Libland buys a lot of oil.
11. Libland buys a few cars.
12. Libland buys a lot of cotton.
13. Libland buys a lot of wool.
14. Libland buys a little iron.
15. Libland doesn't buy much iron.
16. Libland doesn't buy any wine.
17. Libland doesn't buy many cars.

Word Families 2

Page 48

Language: speak, understand, pronounce, mean
Signs: entrance, exit, pull, push
Picnic Places: lake, hill, fields, beach
Occupations: nurse, dentist, shop assistant, student
Hotel: single room, double room, bill, reception
Shopping: try on, size, nylon, how much?

Opposites 3

Page 49

1. Come in and go out
2. Win and lose
3. Ask and answer
4. Sleep and wake up
5. Put on and take off
6. Go to bed and get up

Categories Quiz 2

Page 50

1b, 2a, 3b, 4c, 5b, 6c, 7a, 8b, 9c

Hands

Page 51

1. turn on
2. drive
3. steal
4. wash
5. buy
6. write
7. make
8. break
9. turn off
10. cut

Quick Service

Page 52

Order No. 1: roast pork and peas
Order No. 2: ham salad and bread roll
Order No. 3: spaghetti with tomato sauce
Order No. 4: grilled lamb, mushrooms and peas
Order No. 5: strawberries and cream
Order No. 6: boiled beef, carrots and cabbage
Order No. 7: fried bacon and sausages
Order No. 8: vanilla ice-cream and pears

Around the World

Page 53

1. Norway
2. Wales
3. Argentina
4. Cyprus
5. Denmark
7. Thailand
6. Portugal
8. Panama
9. New Zealand
10. Turkey
11. United States
12. Sweden

Doubles 3

Page 54

ashtray, matchbox, upstairs, grandchild, bookshop, tape recorder, night-club, doorstep, postman, headache, businessman

Sports

Page 55

Individuals: 4. waterskiing 5. fishing 7. running 8. ice-skating 13. shooting 17. skiing 18. diving

2 or more people: 1. squash 2. table tennis 6. snooker 10. tennis 12. boxing 16. badminton

Teams: 3. baseball 9. rugby 11. cricket 14. basketball 15. hockey

Station Signs

Page 56

1. luggage locker
2. facilities for the handicapped
3. left luggage
4. luggage trolleys
5. information
6. car rental
7. non-smokers
8. public telephone
9. lost property
10. toilets and washroom
11. cafeteria
12. buffet
13. drinking water
14. meeting point
15. waiting room

Word Families 3

Page 57

1. saucer, pot, dish, pan
2. socialist, party member, minister, communist
3. operator, directory, dial, call box
4. wound, injury, disease, fever
5. gale, thunderstorm, lightning, frost
6. pair, couple, billion, dozen

Map Reading

Page 58

1. canal
2. coast
3. bridge
4. farmland
5. castle
6. stone circle
7. forest
8. footpath
9. old wall
10. motorway
11. village
12. ferry

The Application Form

Page 59

1. Family name
2. Mr/Mrs/Miss/Ms
3. First name
4. Date of birth
5. Place of birth
6. Marital status
7. Children
8. Present address
9. Tel. no.
10. Education: schools attended
11. Education: university/college
12. Previous experience
13. Present position
14. Present salary
15. Languages spoken
16. Driving licence
17. Interests
18. Names and addresses of 2 referees
19. Date available
20. Date
21. Signature

A Picnic in the Country

Page 60

	True	False
1. Someone's reading.	X	
2. Someone's swimming.		X
3. Someone's driving.		X
4. Someone's climbing.	X	
5. Someone's drinking.		X
6. Someone's riding.		X
7. Someone's resting.	X	
8. Someone's fighting.	X	
9. Someone's jumping.	X	
10. Someone's sewing.	X	
11. Someone's crying.	X	
12. Someone's shaving.		X
13. Someone's hurrying.		X
14. Someone's laughing.		X
15. Someone's hiding.	X	
16. Someone's standing.	X	
17. Someone's leaving.		X
18. Someone's shooting.		X
19. Someone's watching.	X	
20. Someone's running.		X

Abbreviations 3

Page 61

BA – Bachelor of Arts
MA – Master of Arts
Ph.D – Doctor of Philosophy
Dip. – Diploma
Prof. – Professor
Univ. – University
max. – maximum
min. – minimum
VAT – value added tax
vol. – volume
maths. – mathematics
BA – British Airways
Capt. – Captain
m.p.h. – miles per hour
m.p.g. – miles per gallon
Eng. – England
govt. – government
HQ – Headquarters
Ltd. – Limited
Co. – Company
EEC – European Economic Community
         (Common Market)

Opposites 4

Page 62

smooth – rough
soft – hard
thick – thin
pleasant – unpleasant
simple – difficult
sweet – bitter
strong – weak
soft – loud
comfortable – uncomfortable
safe – dangerous
interesting – boring
antique – modern
fine – rainy

Crossword 4

Page 63

Hotel Signs

Page 64

1. Ring for service
2. Messages for guests
3. Check in here
4. Luggage
5. Laundry
6. Porter
7. Lounge
8. Tours
9. Roof garden
10. Manager
11. Please do not disturb
12. Swimming pool

Word List

The numbers beside each word are the page numbers where the word is used in a game. If the word is used often, you will see the first three page numbers followed by ...

A

a.m. (ante meridiem)   18, 45
abbreviation   18, 34, 50 ...
about   32, 45
above   63
across   8, 27, 44 ...
AD (anno Domini)   34
address   59
adjective   22, 42
aeroplane   39
again   13
against   63
airport   13, 39
Alaska   32
album   7
all   8, 14, 16 ...
alone   55
also   41
always   40
ambulance   43
among   63
answer   27, 39, 44 ...
antique   62
any   46
apple   6
application   59
April   41, 45
Arabic   45
Argentina   53
arm   24, 27
around   53
arrive   31
art   59
ashtray   54
ask   25, 49
assistant   59
astronomy   59
at   41, 45
attended   59
August   41
Australia   36
Australian   36
available   59
Avenue (Ave)   34

B

Bachelor of Arts (BA)   61
back (adv)   26, 36
back (n)   24, 27
bacon   52
badly   40
badminton   55
ball   23
banana   11, 50

bank   12
bar   16, 25
baseball   55
basketball   55
bathroom   9, 30
BC (before Christ)   34
beach   48
bean   29
bed   10
bedroom   9, 10, 30
beef   52
beer   11, 29
before   18, 25
behind   63
Belgium   42
below   63
beside   22, 63
between   63
bicycle   13
big   42
bill   26, 48
billion   57
bird   21
birth   59
birthday   45
biscuit   11, 29
bitter   62
black   8
blank   36
blanket   10
blouse   14
blue   8
boat   23
body   27, 50
boiled   52
book (n)   17, 23, 43
book (v)   26, 45
bookshop   54
boring   62
boss   43
bottle   23, 29, 43
box   19
boxing   55
boy   39
branch   8
Brazil   36, 45
Brazilian   36
bread   6, 29, 52
break (broken)   24, 51
breakfast   25
bridge   58
bring (brought)   29
Britain   41
British Airways (BA)   61
brother   7
brown   8

Brussels   42
buffet   56
burn (burnt)   24
bus (buses)   19, 28
bus station   19
business   36
businessman   54
busy   60
butter   6, 45
buy   45, 46, 51
by   13

C

cabbage   52
café   11, 12
cafeteria   56
cake   11, 29
call box   57
camera   14
camping site   12, 19
can (n)   29
can (v)   10, 14, 16
Canada   36
Canadian   36
canal   58
capital   36
Captain (Capt)   61
car   23, 28, 46 ...
carpet   10
carrot   52
carry   52
castle   58
cat   21
category(ies)   39, 50
chair   21, 33
change (v)   25, 26
cheap   22
check in (v)   64
check-out   25
cheese   6, 11, 29
cheque book   23
chicken   11
child (children)   28, 38, 59
chips   11
chocolate   11
Christmas   41
church   12
cigarette   26
cinema   35, 45
circle   26
city(ies)   36
class   45
clean   15
clearly   59
climb   60

close (closed) 16
clothes 50
cloud 8
cloudy 32
coast 58
coat 14
coffee 11, 39, 46
coffee-pot 30
cold (n) 24
colour 8, 39
college 59
column 55
comb 28
come 31, 45
come in 49
comfortable 62
Common Market (EEC) 61
communist 57
Company (Co) 61
connect 63
cook (cooking) 20
correct 16, 18, 19
correctly 53
cotton 46
count 21
country (ies) 32, 39, 46
couple 57
craft 59
cream 52
cricket 55
crossword 8, 27, 44 …
cruzeiro 37
cry 60
cup 10
cut 24, 51
cycle (cycling) 38
Cyprus 53

D

dance (dancing) 20, 31
danger 16
dangerous 62
dark 22
date 39, 59
daughter 21, 43
day 11, 33, 39 …
dear 50
December 34, 41, 50
Denmark 53
dentist 48
department 59
departure lounge 19
describe 32
design 59
dial 25, 57
different 32, 35, 43 …
difficult 42, 62
dining room 9
dinner 25
Diploma (Dip) 59, 61
director 59
directory 57
disease 57
dish (es) 52, 57
dislike 62

disturb (please do not disturb) 64
diving 55
do 38, 41, 45 …
don't 14
Doctor + name (Dr) 34, 50
Doctor of Philosophy (PhD) 61
doctor 25, 43
dog 7, 21, 26
dollar 36
doorstep 54
double room 25, 48
down 8, 16, 27
dozen 57
drachma 36
dress 14
drink 11, 39, 45 …
drinking water 56
drinks (n) 25
drive (driving) 20, 26, 51 …
driving licence 59
dry 32

E

each 16
ear 27
early 25, 40
easy 42
eat (eating) 11, 15
education 59
egg 43
Egypt 36
Egyptian 36
eight 12
eleven 44
emergency 25
end 41
England 45, 61
English 45
entrance 48
European Economic Community (EEC) 61
every 25
everything 10
exit 48
expensive 22
experience 59
explain 56
eye 27

F

facilities 56
factory (ies) 28, 35
fall 24
false 60
family (ies) 9, 48, 57 …
family name 59
farm 39
farmer 21
farmland 58
fast 42
fat 42
father 7
February 41
ferry 58

fever 57
(a) few (fewest) 41, 46
field 13, 48
fight 60
fill in 24, 36, 45
find 18, 22, 31 …
fine 62
finger 24, 50
finish 17, 59
first 19, 41, 44
first name 39, 59
fish 6, 50
fishing 55
floor 19
flower 28
fly (n) 21, 39
fly (v) 26, 31
fog 32
food 11, 50
foot (feet) 27, 28
football 21, 30, 45
football match 26
footpath 58
foreign 20
forest 58
forget 14
fork 10, 33
form 59
forty 44
four 44
franc 36
France 36, 39, 45
free 20, 25, 45
French 36, 45, 59
Friday (Fri) 18, 45
fridge 10
fried 52
friend 45
from 30, 41, 43
frost 57
fruit 50

G

gale 57
gallon 43
game 15, 26, 31
garage 9
garden 9, 64
gas 46
GB (Great Britain) 18, 42
German 36, 59
Germany 36
get up 40, 49
girl 41, 59
give 15
glass (glasses) 28, 46
go 13, 31, 45
go out 49
go to bed 49
gold 46
golf 55
good 45
got 24
government (govt) 61
grandfather 7

grandmother 7
grass 8
Greece 36
Greek 36
green 8
grey 8
grilled 52
ground floor 19
group 57
guest 25, 65
guide 21

H

haircut 30
half 44
ham 52
hand 24, 27, 43 …
handicapped 56
happen 23, 45
happy 24
hard (difficult) 62
hard (soft) 42
hat 14, 23, 43
have 20
he 23, 24, 36 …
head 27, 43
headache 54
headquarters (HQ) 61
heart 27
heating 33
heavy 22
hello 9
help 10, 23, 33
her 14, 40
here 22, 42
hers 23
hide (hidden) 31, 60
high 22
hill 48
him 24, 40
his 13, 23, 34 …
hockey 55
holiday 14, 23, 39 …
home 29
horse 21
hospital 35
hot 32
hotel 23, 33, 48 …
hotel room 26
hour 45
house 10
how 40
how much 48
hungry 24
hurry 45, 60

I

ice 24
ice-cream 11, 30, 52
ice-skating 55
ill 24
in 11, 14, 18 …
India 32
individual 55

information 56
injury 57
insect 39
inside 63
interest (n) 20, 59
interesting 62
Ireland 36
Irish 36
iron 46
island 28
it 14, 25
Italian 36
Italy 36
its 41

J

jacket 14
January 41
Japan 36
Japanese 36
jeans 14
job 39, 50, 59
journalist 23
juice 19
July 41, 59
jump 60
June 41

K

key 23, 33
kilogram (kg) 18, 29
kilometre (km) 18
kitchen 9, 10, 39
knife (knives) 10, 28, 33
know 38
kick-off 45

L

lake 48
lamb 52
language 20, 39, 45 …
last 36
late 40
laugh 60
laundry 65
lb (pound weight) 18
leaf (leaves) 28
learn (learning) 20
leather 46
leave (left) 31, 36, 60
left (adj) 38
left luggage 56
leg 21
letter (alphabet) 41
letter 13, 26, 43
lift 33
light (adj) (not dark) 22
light (adj) (not heavy) 22
light (n) 33
lightning 57
like 32, 62
Limited (Ltd) 61
lira (lire) 36

list 6, 10, 14 …
listen (listening) 15, 20
litre 43
(a) little 40, 46, 59
livingroom 30
loaf 29
locker 56
London 36
long (longest) 41
look at 6, 12, 13 …
lose 49
lost property office 16, 56
(a) lot (of) 40, 46
loud 62
lounge 64
low 22
luggage 56, 64
lunch 25

M

magazine 43, 59
make 10, 19, 30
man 50 …
manager 65
many 19, 20, 30 …
map 12, 23, 36 …
March 36, 39, 41
marital 59
mark 36
market 35
married 50
Master of Arts (MA) 61
matchbox 54
mathematics (maths) 61
matter 24
maximum (max.) 61
May 41, 45
me 7
meal 39, 50
mean 48
meat 6
medicine 43
meeting point 56
message 13, 65
metre (m) 18
Mexican 36
Mexico 36
midday 25
miles per gallon (m.p.g.) 61
miles per hour (m.p.h.) 61
milk 6
million 42
minimum (min.) 61
minister 57
Miss 59
missing 24, 33
modern 62
Monday (Mon) 18, 45
money 23, 36, 50
month 39, 41
morning 18
mother 7
motorbike 13, 30
motorway 58
mountain 50

mountain climbing   59
mouth   27
Mr   21, 33, 36 …
Mrs   21, 33, 59
Ms   59
much   46
mushrooms   52
music   20, 45
mustard   43
my   45

N

name (n)   19, 39, 41 …
name (v)   36
nationality   39, 50
NB (nota bene)   34
never   40
New Zealand   53
new   10, 22, 59
news   45
newspaper   43
next to   39, 50, 63
night   8, 25
night-club   54
nine   44
ninety   44
no   33, 38
No Entry   38
No Stopping   38
noisy   22
non-smoker   56
none   59
noon   18
north (N)   18
northeast (NE)   18
Norway   53
nose   27
not   50
notebook   23
November   41
number   19, 21, 22 …
nurse   48
nylon   48

O

object   26
occupation   48
October   41
office   35, 64
oil   46
old (not new)   22, 58
old (not young)   35
omelette   11
on   13, 24, 32 …
once   44
one   9, 10, 18 …
only   25, 45
open   16, 25
operator   57
opposite   49, 62, 63
orange (adj)   8
orange (n)   8, 19
orange juice   11, 19
order (n)   52

others   43
out   45
outside   63
over   63

P

p.m. (post meridiem)   25, 45
packet   29
pain   24
pair   14, 22, 49 …
pan   57
Panama   53
park   12
parking (P)   25, 34
part   27, 30, 50
party   45
party member   57
passport   14
pay   26
pea   52
pear   52
pen   23
pence (p)   34
people   32, 42, 52
pepper   43
person   39, 40
peseta   36
peso   36
phone (v)   9
photography   59
picnic   38, 48, 60
picture   22, 31, 42
piece   29
pillow   10, 33
pint   43
place   10, 12, 16 …
plane   13, 26
plate   10
platform   16
play (playing)   20
pleasant   62
please   9, 45, 59
please turn over (PTO)   18
plural   28
police station   12
policeman (men)   28
pork   52
porter   64
Portugal   53
position (job)   59
position   63
post office   35
postcard   30, 43
postman   54
pot   57
potato (es)   6
pound (lb)   18
pound (£)   36
prefer   40
present (adj.)   59
previous   59
Professor (Prof.)   61
programme   32, 45
pronounce   48
PS (Postcript)   34

public telephone   56
pull   48
pullover   14
push   48
put   6, 10, 16 …
put on   49

Q

quarter   44
question   45
quick   11, 52
quickly   40
quiet   22
quiz   39, 40, 50

R

rabbit   63
radio   23, 25, 45
railway station   56
rain   32
rainy   62
read (reading)   13, 20, 40 …
reception   25, 48
recognise   53
red   8
referee   59
remember   16
rental (car rental)   56
represent   58
rest   60
restaurant   12, 25
rice   11
ride   31, 60
right (not left)   38
right (not wrong)   10, 21, 42
ring (for service)   64
river   43, 50
riyal   36
road (Rd)   34, 38, 43
roast   11, 52
roll   52
roof   65
room   9, 14, 56
rough   62
round   32
rugby   55
run   31, 60
running   55
Russian   50

S

safe   62
salad   52
salary   59
salt   43
same   21, 23
sandwich   11
Saturday (Sat)   18, 45
sauce   52
saucer   57
Saudi   36
Saudi Arabia   36
sausage   52

say 23, 24
scene 60
school 45, 59
Scotland 32
sea 8, 50
season 40
second 44
secret 13
see 14, 40
sell 46
send 26
September 41
service 25, 52
sew 60
shave 60
she 9, 23
sheep 38
sheet 10
ship 46
shoot 54, 60
shop 39
shop assistant 48
shopping 48
shopping list 6, 19
short (shortest) 41, 42
show 12, 25, 37
sign 16, 38, 48 ...
signature 59
simple 62
sing 15
single 59
single room 48
singular 28
sister 7
sit 15
site 38
sitting room 9
six 44
sixteen 44
size 48
ski 55
sleep 40, 49
slow 42
slowly 40
small 42, 46
smoke 26
smoker 56
smooth 62
snooker 55
snow 8, 32
socialist 57
socks 14
soft 42, 62
soldier 41
someone 60
sometimes 8
son 7, 43
sort 40
sound 45
soup 11
south (S) 34
Southwest (SW) 34
spaghetti 52
Spain 36, 59
Spanish 36, 59
speak 48

spell 53
spend (spent) 37
spoken 59
spoon 10
sport 39, 50, 55
spring 36
spy 13
square (sq) 31, 34, 43
squash 55
stamp 43
stand 60
start 41
station 13, 16, 19 ...
status 59
stay 23, 33
steal 51
stomach 27
stone 58
stop 15
stopping 38
story 45
strange 53
strawberry 52
street (St) 34, 43
strong 62
student 41, 48
subject 57
sugar 29
summer 40, 59
sun 8
Sunday (Sun) 18, 45
sunglasses 23
sunny 32, 33
sunset 8
supermarket 35, 39
surname 39, 50
Sweden 53
sweet (adj.) 62
swim (swimming) 31, 50, 60
swimming pool 64
Swiss 36
Switzerland 36

T

table 21
table tennis 55
take 13, 41
take off 49
talk 15
tall 42
tape recorder 54
taxi 13, 16, 43
tea 11, 29
teacher 39, 59
team 21, 55
teapot 10
telephone (Tel) 16, 19, 34
telephone box 19
telephone number 19, 59
television (TV) 20, 43, 25
tell 25
ten 44
tennis 55
Thailand 53
theatre 45

their 21, 48
them 9
then 13
there 9, 13, 16
there is 32, 33
these 38, 48
they 11
thick 62
thin 42
thin 62
think 15
third 44
thirsty 24
thirteen 44
this 12, 31, 45
thunderstorm 57
Thursday (Thurs) 45
ticket 14, 45
ticket office 16, 35
tights 14
till 25
time 45, 50
tired 24
today 32
toilet 16, 34, 56
tomato 52
tooth (teeth) 27, 28
toothbrush 30
toothpaste 30
total 21
tour 64
tourist 21
towel 23, 33
town 12
traffic lights 38
train 13, 39
travel centre 16
traveller's cheques 25, 26, 43
tree 8
trip 36
trolley 56
trousers 50
truck 26
true 60
try on 48
Tuesday (Tues) 45
Turkey 53
turn 38
turn off 51
turn on 51
TV (television) 32, 34
twelve 44
twice 44
two 19, 44
type 59

U

uncomfortable 62
under 63
underground 13
understand 48
underwear 14
Union of Soviet Socialist Republics
 (USSR) 18
United Kingdom (UK) 18

United Nations (UN) 18
United States of America (USA) 18, 53
University (Univ.) 59, 61
unpleasant 62
up 25, 36
upstairs 54
us 25
usually 55

V

Value Added Tax (VAT) 61
vanilla 52
vegetable 50
verb 31, 41, 49
village 58
visit (visited) 36
volume (vol.) 61

W

wait 13, 15
waiter 52
waiting room 16, 56
wake up 49
wake-up (n) 25
Wales 53
walk (walking) 12, 20, 31 ...
wall 58
wash 51
washroom 56
watch (watches) (n) 28
watch (watching) (v) 20, 32, 60
water 23, 33, 56
water-skiing 55
way 12, 36
way out 16
WC 34
weak 62
weather 32
Wednesday (Wed) 45
week (wk) 34, 45
weekend 30
well 40
went (past of go) 12, 36
what 11, 23, 24
when 17, 35, 40
where 9, 13, 35
which 40, 43
white 8
who 7
why 24
wife 7, 43, 50
win 26, 49
wind 32
wine 11, 29
winter 40
with 19, 30, 48
woman (women) 28, 45, 50
wood 46
wool 46
word 19, 22, 24 ...
work (n) 38, 40
work (v) 35
world 32, 36, 45

wound 57
write 16, 20, 22
write out 61
wrong 42

Y

year (yr) 34
yellow 8
yen 36
yes 14
you 14, 18, 21 ...
young (younger) 22, 35
your 51
yours 45

Z

zero 44